WHALES AND DOLPHINS

QUESTIONS
AND
ANSWERS

Text: Éva Plagányi
Consultant: Dr Vic Cockcroft
Illustrations: David Thorpe

NEW
HOLLAND

FIN WHALE

FRASER'S DOLPHIN

Contents

4. Discovering whales and dolphins

6. Identifying whales and dolphins

8. Whales and their whereabouts

10. Living in water

12. In the deep

14. Finding the way

16. Finding food

18. Hunters of the high seas

20. Sounds of the sea

22. Raising a family

24. Living together

26. Living with others

28. Whale winners

30. Save the whale!

32. Index

First published in 1994 by
New Holland (Publishers) Ltd
London • Cape Town • Sydney

Copyright © 1994 in text: Éva Plagányi
Copyright © 1994 New Holland (Publishers) Ltd

ISBN 1 85368 349 3

New Holland (Publishers) Ltd
37 Connaught Street, London W2 2AZ

Editor Sean Fraser
Designer Tracey Mackenzie
Illustrator David Thorpe

Typesetting by Tracey Mackenzie
Reproduction by Unifoto (Pty) Ltd
Printed and bound in Singapore by
Kyodo Printing Co (Pte) Ltd

Introduction

Whales and dolphins are a group of mammals called cetaceans that spend their entire lives in water. Their ancestors may have been hoofed land animals which hunted fishes in shallow water about 60 million years ago. These animals slowly adapted to life in water and today there are at least 79 different species of cetaceans, living in all the world's oceans from the chilly Arctic in the north to the Antarctic in the south. There are two very different groups of cetaceans: baleen whales, such as the blue and humpback whales, have two blowholes and long plates of baleen which look like giant combs and hang from the roof of their mouths; toothed whales, such as the sperm whales, killer whales and dolphins, all have only a single blowhole and proper teeth. Whales and dolphins are some of the most intelligent and mysterious creatures alive today.

Can you identify these whales and dolphins? The answers are on page 32.

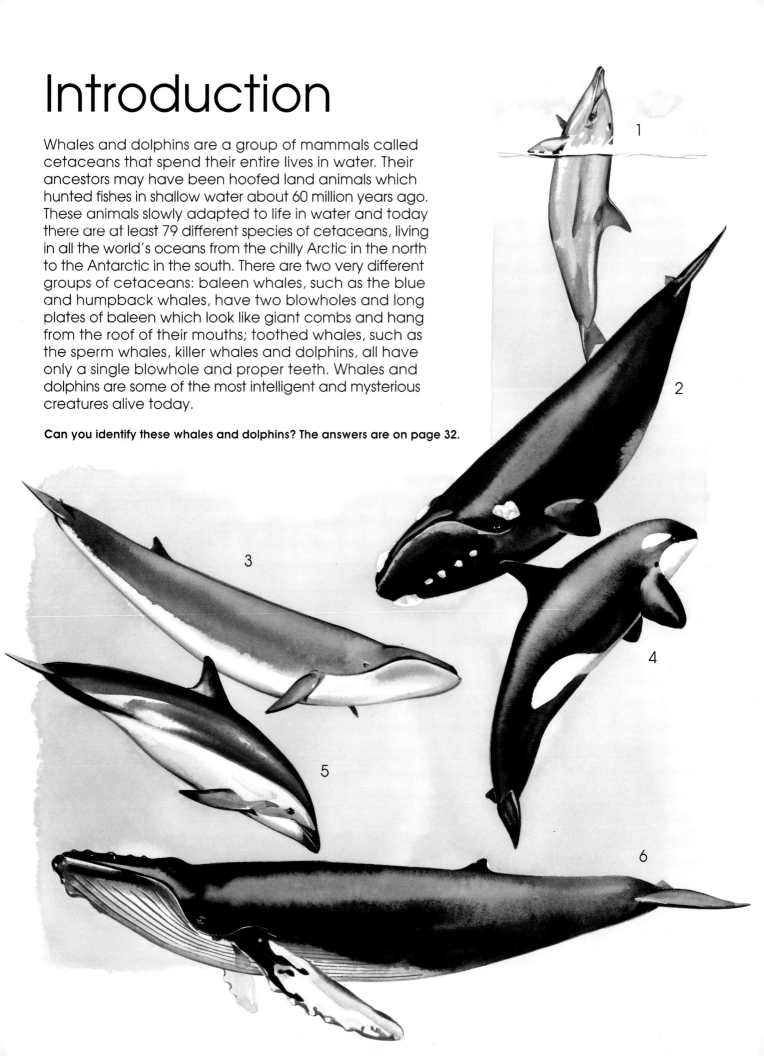

BOTTLENOSE DOLPHIN

Discovering whales and dolphins

Cetaceans are mammals – just as humans are. They are warm blooded, breathe air and give birth to live young which they suckle, care for and teach. Man has always been fascinated by these gentle giants but scientists are still puzzling over the many mysteries surrounding these fascinating creatures.

Why are whales and dolphins like torpedoes?

Because, like fish, they need to be streamlined to make it easier for them to move through the water. For the same reason, whales and dolphins have almost no body hair at all, and they do not have any body parts like ear lobes which stick out and slow them down when swimming. Also, their mammary glands and genital organs are tucked away in special slits in the skin. To make them better swimmers, their forelimbs have developed over many thousands of years into paddle-shaped flippers and, except for a few small bones which remain, they have completely lost their back legs. To propel themselves through the water, they have a tail which forms a huge fluke. The main difference between cetaceans and other mammals is that whales and dolphins spend their whole lives in water. The only other mammals which do so are dugongs and manatees. Other species, such as seals, spend much of their lives at sea, but have to return to land to breed.

STREAMLINED FRASER'S DOLPHIN

Are dolphins really so clever?

Yes, but because they live in a different world to ours, they are 'clever' in a very different way to us. Their brains are certainly big and complex like human brains, which suggests that they are very intelligent. Animals in captivity can be taught fairly easily to perform amusing tricks. Part of the reason why they seem so clever is that they use a very advanced system of echolocation (see page 14) which allows them to do things we could only do with the help of special equipment. But no-one is quite sure how intelligent cetaceans really are.

CROSS-SECTION THROUGH A WHALE'S SKIN

Why are whales fat?

To keep warm! Whales do not have thick hairy coats and cannot curl up or huddle together like other mammals to keep warm. Instead they have developed a thick layer of fat, called blubber, under the skin. This layer is their warm coat and can be up to half a metre thick! Blubber is also important for storing fuel which the whale needs in the months when it does not feed.

MOBY DICK

Did you know?

The only whale which could ever have swallowed Jonah in the biblical story, is the huge sperm whale. It is the only whale with a throat big enough to swallow a man whole. Although the blue whale is much bigger, its throat is too small!

Are dolphins and porpoises different?

Many people refer to dolphins as porpoises, but there are in fact only six true porpoises in the world. Porpoises are different because they have spade-shaped teeth, while dolphins have cone-shaped teeth. Porpoises are not common in African waters, except for the harbour porpoise which occurs widely in the northern hemisphere. The finless porpoise which lives in waters off south-east Asia is quaint because it does not have a dorsal fin and has a parrot-like 'beak'.

What was Moby Dick?

He was a great white sperm whale in a famous novel called *Moby Dick*, written by Herman Melville in the nineteenth century. In the book, Moby Dick is chased across the seas by the bitter captain of a whaling ship who is seeking revenge against the whale which caused him to lose his leg. The book ends sadly with a three day battle between Moby Dick and the hunters. In the end only one man survives the battle.

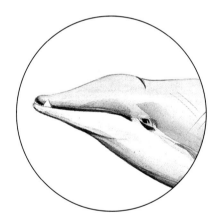

HECTOR'S BEAKED WHALE

Are dolphins whales?

All dolphins are toothed whales, but belong to a completely different group to the baleen whales and sperm whales. The dolphin family includes large dolphins like the killer whale and pilot whales, which are only called whales because they are so big. This can be quite confusing as even the much smaller melon-headed whale is really a dolphin and not a whale at all!

Have we met all the world's cetaceans?

Maybe not. Beaked whales, such as Arnoux's and Hector's beaked whales, are the least known of all the cetaceans because they live far out to sea in the very depths of the oceans. Some of these strange creatures have never been seen alive and the only reason why we know they exist is because dead animals have been washed ashore. There may even be unknown species of beaked whales, and perhaps other cetaceans too, living in the deep ocean waiting to be discovered!

MELON-HEADED WHALE

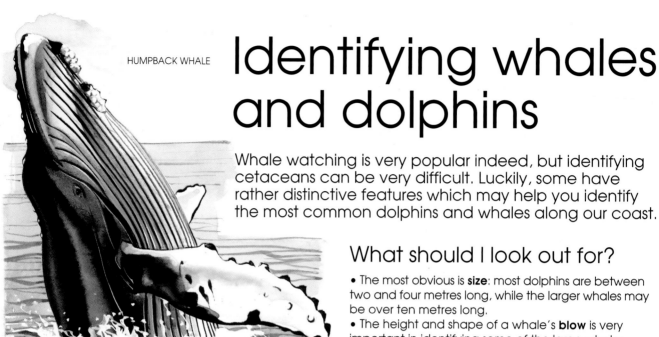

HUMPBACK WHALE

Identifying whales and dolphins

Whale watching is very popular indeed, but identifying cetaceans can be very difficult. Luckily, some have rather distinctive features which may help you identify the most common dolphins and whales along our coast.

What should I look out for?

• The most obvious is **size**: most dolphins are between two and four metres long, while the larger whales may be over ten metres long.
• The height and shape of a whale's **blow** is very important in identifying some of the large whales. Remember too that baleen whales have two blowholes while toothed whales have only one.
• The size and position of the **dorsal fin**. Pilot whales have a distinctive broad-based dorsal fin far down on their back. Right whale dolphins are named after right whales because, like the whales, they do not have a dorsal fin. The Indo-Pacific humpback dolphin really does have a hump on its back – and a dorsal fin on top of that. Its long snout also appears first when it surfaces.
• Whether or not the whale flips its **tail** into the air just before it dives is a tell-tale sign.
• The **number** and **behaviour** of individuals in a **group**.
• Dolphins such as striped and spotted dolphins can easily be told from the **patterns** on their bodies.

Which whale blows to the side?

The sperm whale blows forwards and to the left side because its unusual blowhole is on the top left hand side of the head. This old 'big head' has an almost rectangular appearance in water. In contrast, the stocky southern right whale has a V-shaped blow and a characteristic 'bonnet' of white callosites on its head. The humpback whale has a blow rather like a balloon, but is most easily identified by its huge white under-flippers and the white underside of its tail flukes. These three whales all flip their tails into the air before diving.

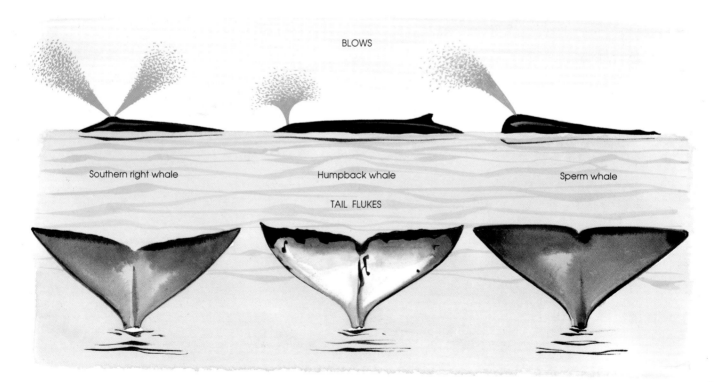

BLOWS

Southern right whale · Humpback whale · Sperm whale

TAIL FLUKES

Is it a dolphin or is it a shark?

It is actually quite easy to tell whether a fin peeping out of the water belongs to a shark or a dolphin. Dolphins must come to the surface to breathe at regular intervals and so their dorsal fin moves up and down in the water. Sharks don't perform this 'porpoising' motion and so their dorsal fin doesn't bounce up and down at the surface! The grey bottlenose dolphin, which is often seen surfing on breaking waves close inshore, is sometimes mistaken for a shark.

FIN OF A BOTTLENOSE DOLPHIN

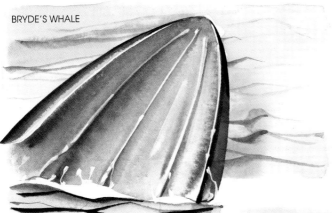
BRYDE'S WHALE

Which whale has three ridges on its head?

Bryde's whale (pronounced *broodis* whale). These long, thin whales are bluish-grey and are sometimes confused with sei whales. But Bryde's whales have two extra ridges on the head and their small, pointed dorsal fin is not visible when they blow. Bryde's whales are about 14 metres long and their blow is tall and thin. They arch their backs when they dive and their tail flukes are not usually visible.

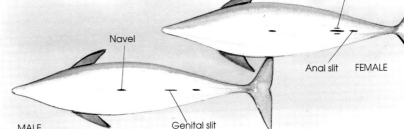

Mammary slit

Navel

Anal slit   FEMALE

MALE

Genital slit

Did you know?

Heaviside's dolphin was named after the wrong man! A museum thought that a Captain Heaviside had collected the first specimen, but in fact it was another man, called Captain Haviside. By the time the mistake was discovered, it was too late to change the dolphin's name!

How do we tell the difference between a male and a female cetacean?

Male and female cetaceans usually look very similar. Their reproductive organs are hidden inside special slits, but the genital slit of the female is much closer to the anus than it is in the male. But it is much easier to tell killer whales apart. The male's dorsal fin, which can be almost 1,8 metres tall, is nearly twice as tall and much straighter than the female's and, like sperm whales, male killer whales are much bigger than the females.

COMMON DOLPHIN

Which dolphin has a beautiful criss-cross pattern?

More slender than bottlenose dolphins, common dolphins are unmistakable because of the criss-cross figure of eight along their sides. They have a large sickle-shaped dorsal fin, enjoy bow-riding and may sometimes gather in enormous schools. The slightly smaller dusky dolphin is sometimes seen leaping about in the waves just offshore. They have a very distinctive dorsal fin which is black in front and lighter behind.

Whales and their whereabouts

Some whales and dolphins are found in oceans around the world, but others are more fussy about where they live. Some move around quite a lot and may visit the same places every year, travelling many thousands of kilometres from their winter homes to their summer homes and back again. These journeys are called migrations.

SOUTHERN RIGHT WHALE

Where can you see whales and dolphins?

The best whale-spotting areas are those which overlook winter nursery grounds or migration routes. Humpback whales, for example, are often seen as they migrate close inshore up South Africa's east coast to breeding grounds off Madagascar, or on stop-overs such as in Hervey Bay, Australia. Dolphins are seen almost anywhere, and friendly dolphins regularly swim with people at Monkey Mia on Shark Bay, off Dingle in western Ireland and in the Bahamas.

Which whales are spotted most often?

Southern right whales are commonly seen off the southern-most parts of South America, Australia and South Africa. Humpback whales are also frequently spotted from the land as they migrate up and down the coasts of Australia, and also along the east coasts of South Africa and North America. Off the west coast of North America, people flock in their thousands to see grey whales. Bryde's whales are a big attraction off Ogata in Japan. Lucky observers sometimes catch a glimpse of a sperm whale or even a killer whale, but they are only commonly seen off Kaikoura, New Zealand; and Vancouver Island, Canada, respectively.

WHALEWATCHING HOT-SPOTS

Can dolphins survive in fresh water?

Yes, there are five different species of freshwater dolphins which live in large rivers in Asia and South America. The marine Indo-Pacific humpback dolphin is able to survive in both salt water and brackish water and some-times feeds in estuaries. Like other dolphins, freshwater dolphins are thought to have evolved in the sea.

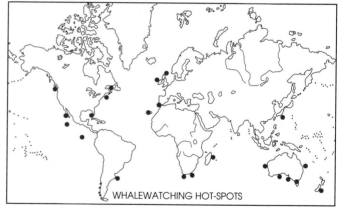

INDO-PACIFIC HUMPBACK DOLPHIN

HEAVISIDE'S DOLPHIN

Why do some areas have so many whales and dolphins?

Thirty-seven kinds of cetaceans have been recorded in southern African waters, while over 40 species occur in Australian waters. One of the main reasons why such a variety is found here is the difference in water temperature around the coast. While some cetaceans may be found in cold waters, others prefer warm tropical seas. The west coast of southern Africa is fed by a cold current from the Antarctic region, while the water on the east coast is relatively warm. Australia has warm waters in the north but cooler waters in the south.

Do some dolphins have smaller home ranges than others?

Yes. Although some species such as killer whales, common dolphins and bottlenose dolphins are found in almost all parts of the world, others live in only small parts of the world's oceans. Heaviside's dolphin lives in the cold Benguela current off the west coast of South Africa and Namibia, and is not found anywhere else in the world. Hector's dolphin lives only in the waters around New Zealand. Both these small dolphins occur close inshore.

HUMPBACK WHALE

BRYDE'S WHALE

Do whales migrate?

Yes, they do. Many whales, such as the humpback whale, spend the summer in Antarctic waters. During these months the animals they feed on appear in their millions and so a grand feast is laid on for the hungry whales! As the Antarctic winter approaches and ice forms on the water, the whales move north to the warmer waters off the coast of Africa and elsewhere. Here they mate, give birth and raise their young without having to worry about trying to keep warm. In the spring they move south again to Antarctica. This is why we see so many whales off the coasts of southern Africa in winter.

Who doesn't like the cold at all?

Bryde's whale. Unlike other members of its group, this whale never ventures into the cold Antarctic waters but spends its days instead in warmer waters. Two different populations occur off southern Africa: one form is a rover and feeds mainly on plankton quite far out to sea, while a smaller form feeds on small fishes and lives nearer to the coast.

Living in water

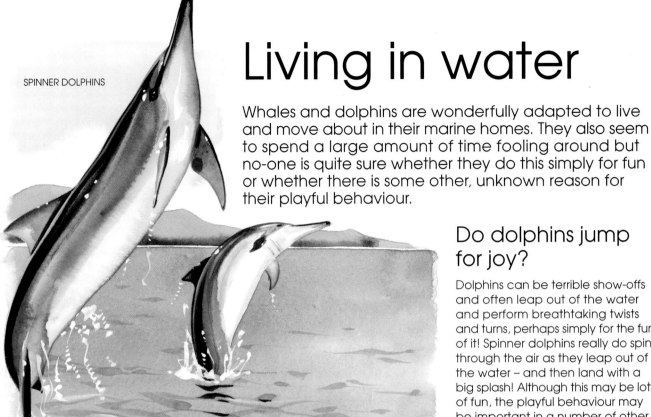

SPINNER DOLPHINS

Whales and dolphins are wonderfully adapted to live and move about in their marine homes. They also seem to spend a large amount of time fooling around but no-one is quite sure whether they do this simply for fun or whether there is some other, unknown reason for their playful behaviour.

Do dolphins jump for joy?

Dolphins can be terrible show-offs and often leap out of the water and perform breathtaking twists and turns, perhaps simply for the fun of it! Spinner dolphins really do spin through the air as they leap out of the water – and then land with a big splash! Although this may be lots of fun, the playful behaviour may be important in a number of other ways too. Male dolphins sometimes use them to attract females (see page 22) and youngsters practise valuable skills to prepare them for later in life. By leaping low out of the water while swimming, in what is known as 'porpoising', southern right whale dolphins are able to take a breath of air while still moving and keep up high speeds without using too much energy.

Do whales really blow off steam?

When whales blow, they are simply breathing out. The 'steam' is actually water vapour which forms because the warm air in their lungs cools as it meets the colder outside air – just the same as when we breathe out on a cold day! The old whalers cried 'There she blows!' when they saw the beautiful jet of 'steam' so the crew knew immediately that a large whale had been sighted. After a long dive, a big whale blows out with such force that the blow can actually be heard more than a kilometre away, and the whale can take in nearly three thousand times as much air in a single breath as we do! These big breathers are also sometimes accused of having very bad breath! The fishy smell is caused by greasy substances in the lungs and nasal passages.

Why do whales grow so big?

Because they can! It is only in the sea that animals can grow to the massive sizes of the great whales because seawater supports their body. Land animals need strong limbs to move about against the forces of gravity. In the sea, being big also means being cosy. The bigger a whale is, the easier it is to stay warm in cold waters. This is because their large bodies produce more heat than that which is lost through the surface of their bodies.

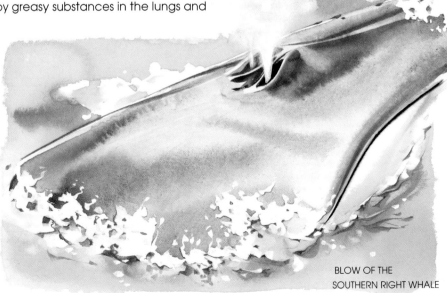

BLOW OF THE
SOUTHERN RIGHT WHALE

TAIL FLUKE OF A SOUTHERN RIGHT WHALE

Can whales sail?

Southern right whales sometimes stand on their heads in the water with only their tails peeping out! As the wind blows against their huge tail flukes, they seem to slowly sail along! Because blood vessels in the flukes are close to the surface, the wind quickly cools down the blood flowing through the flukes so the whale keeps cool in warm waters.

Do cetaceans swim like fish?

No. There are important differences. All cetaceans have a horizontal tail fluke which they move up and down to propel their smooth bodies through the water. Fish have a vertical tail, or caudal fin, which they move from side to side as their scaly bodies swim through the water. Fish also have more fins than whales and dolphins.

Are some whales really pilots?

Pilot whales sometimes swim in a line with one animal at the front which seems to act as the pilot! Sadly, in some northern countries, the pilot is chased into shallow water and when the other pilot whales follow their leader, they are cruelly killed. These whales probably first earned their name because it was believed that they acted just like pilots and guided fishermen to shoals of fish. Dolphins have also been known to pilot ships safely into port. One of the most famous pilots was a Risso's dolphin called 'Pelorus Jack', which, for about 30 years at the beginning of this century, used to guide ships through a dangerous channel in New Zealand.

Did you know?

Cetaceans don't all sleep in the same way we do. Instead, while half their brain is asleep, the other half stays awake and controls their movement and breathing. This ensures that they are always on the lookout and do not drown while they sleep.

LONG-FINNED PILOT WHALE

Why can dolphins swim so fast?

This question has puzzled scientists for many years! Although dolphins are wonderfully streamlined and have large muscles with which they beat their tail flukes up and down, this does still not explain how they can swim so fast. The answer lies in their skin, which is so soft and flexible that it can change shape as the dolphin swims. The water then flows smoothly over the dolphin's body and hardly any 'drag' forces slow it down. Also, their skin secretes an oil which makes it easier for them to 'slip' through the water at high speed! Studies of dolphin skin were even used to improve the efficiency of torpedoes (see page 4).

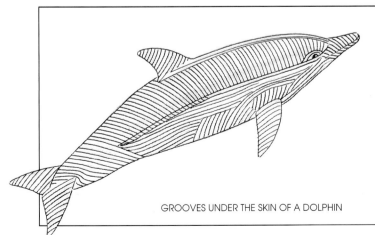
GROOVES UNDER THE SKIN OF A DOLPHIN

SPERM WHALE DIVING

In the deep

Down, down, down, like submarines, the toothed whales swim hundreds of metres into the deep on a single breath of air and hunt prey in waters that are not only cold and dark but also exert tremendous force on their bodies. Although they are mammals just as we are, they have adapted very well to the deep and dark ocean.

How deep can a whale dive?

Different species of whales dive to different depths, but one of the deepest divers is the sperm whale which can dive more than one kilometre, and perhaps even three kilometres, down into the depths of the ocean in search of food! The beaked whales (see page 5) are also very good divers, and some are able to dive as deep as one kilometre. Most of the smaller whales and dolphins don't dive to such great depths. Although bottlenose dolphins, for example, usually don't dive deeper than about 40 metres, they are quite capable of diving down to almost 500 metres!

Can cetaceans ever drown?

Yes, if water enters their lungs they can drown. But healthy cetaceans don't drown because they have a built-in safety valve. In fact, there are a number of complex valves and plugs in the nasal passages leading from the blowhole. These valves close automatically when a cetacean dives so that the water does not flood the airway passages. Nerve endings sense when the blowhole is above water, and it is safe for the whale or dolphin to breathe.

How can huge sperm whales hang motionless in water?

The head has a huge cavity, called the spermaceti organ, which holds over 100 litres of a waxy substance which is very important to the sperm whale. Giant nasal passages run through this organ to the blowhole. By drawing water in through these passages, the whale can change the temperature of the wax in the spermaceti organ! The colder the wax, the denser it becomes, making the whale less buoyant so that it can sink or hang motionless at any depth, ready to pounce on unsuspecting squid. To rise to the surface again, the whale simply blows the water out of its nasal passages, causing the wax to warm up and become less dense. The buoyant whale then floats to the surface without even having to swim!

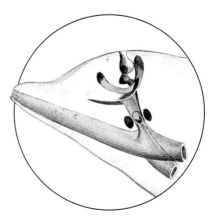

DOLPHIN'S NASAL PASSAGES

SOUTHERN BOTTLENOSE WHALE

How do whales 'hold their breath' for so long?

When humans dive they cannot stay underwater for very long because they soon run out of oxygen and have to come to the surface of the water to breathe. But whales can take down much more oxygen with them because they have more blood in which to store oxygen. They also have many more red blood cells containing haemoglobin which transports oxygen in the blood, and they can store lots of extra oxygen in their muscles! In addition, their heart rate slows down when they dive so that less oxygen is used up. Scientists also suspect that during a deep dive, less oxygen is used because it is only distributed to important organs such as the brain and the heart!

Who can hold their breath the longest?

The bottlenose whales and sperm whales can stay underwater for more than two hours on long dives! Most of the large whales, like the blue and fin whales, rarely stay down for longer than 40 minutes while large dolphins such as the bottlenose dolphin usually stay down for less than 15 minutes. The smaller common dolphin dives for less than three minutes.

What are 'the bends'?

Because all the water above a scuba diver deep down in the ocean creates an enormous amount of pressure on the human body, the air in the diver's blood dissolves. If the diver then rises to the surface too quickly, the nitrogen forms small bubbles in the blood, and can kill a man. This is known as 'the bends', but whales have an extraordinary way of avoiding this. When a whale dives it only takes down one lungful of air which probably doesn't contain enough nitrogen to produce 'the bends'. But it avoids absorbing even this small amount of nitrogen because when the whale dives deeper than about 100 metres, its chest collapses so that the air in the lungs is forced into the passages leading to the blowhole. Nitrogen cannot be absorbed through the passage walls. The lining of the lung walls also becomes thicker so there is even less of a chance of the remaining nitrogen being absorbed.

SCUBA DIVER

Why don't whales get ear-ache when they dive?

Because they have a remarkable adaptation which automatically makes sure that the pressure inside the middle ear is the same as that of the surrounding water! The deeper you dive, the greater is the water pressure, so that if the pressure inside your ear does not increase too, you can get rather painful ear-ache. Humans, of course, can hold their nose and blow underwater, and so 'equalise' the pressure. But in whales the pressure in the middle ear is automatically increased because special tissues inside the ears swell with blood.

Finding the way

Since cetaceans first left the land millions of years ago and made the sea their new home, they have had to adapt to life in water and to the problems of finding their way across the oceans. Toothed whales can hunt and move about in pitch darkness – just as bats do. They have conquered their watery world through an amazing ability to use sound waves rather than light. This extra sense is called echolocation.

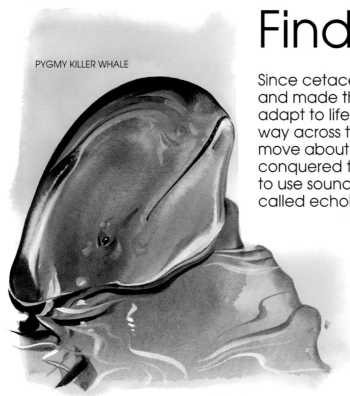

PYGMY KILLER WHALE

Do some whales spy?

Yes, some whales spy on their surroundings! This is called spy-hopping and allows cetaceans like the pygmy killer whale to get a better look at their surroundings. Killer whales spy-hop to scan the tops of floating ice called ice-floes for tasty morsels such as seals! Most cetaceans have good eyesight and can see well both in and out of the water because of a special lens in their eyes which allows them to focus in both environments.

Why are dolphins like warships?

Dolphins use a rather complicated system called echolocation, similar to the way warships find enemy targets. They use the fatty bump or melon on their heads to focus a stream of internally-produced clicking noises as they swim through the water. These sounds bounce back from surrounding objects and the echoes are picked up by special fatty areas on the lower jaw. So the dolphin's jaw 'hears' the sounds and passes them on to the middle ear and brain so that the dolphin can work out what is causing its sound waves to bounce back. In fact, some dolphins are so good at this that they can tell the difference between a ball 45 centimetres wide and one 50 centimetres wide – from a distance of 25 metres!

Why do dolphins 'see with their ears'?

If dolphins relied on eyesight alone, they wouldn't see very much at all because seawater often contains large amounts of sediment and plankton which can make it murky. Also, the deeper the ocean, the darker it becomes, so dolphins and toothed whales use sound rather than light to build a 'picture' of their surroundings. 'Listening' carefully not only allows toothed whales to 'see' on moonless nights and hunt in deep and dark waters, but also allows them to 'see' much further underwater than they ever could with their eyes. This is because sound waves travel much better underwater than do light waves – and about five times faster than they do in air!

STRIPED DOLPHIN

SQUID

Do cetaceans have built-in compasses?

Yes. Whales and dolphins find their way across oceans with the help of an extra sense called biomagnetism, which uses small changes in the Earth's magnetic field to tell them where they are and how long they have been travelling. No-one is sure exactly how they are able to sense changes in the magnetic field, but it seems that sensitive cells in the brain, or in the eyes of some, can pick up these changes.

STRANDED PILOT WHALES

Did you know?

These marine mammals have brains which are highly complex and quite big compared to the rest of their bodies. The cortical layers in their brains are similar to our own, which suggests that they are highly intelligent. The areas of their brain which control communication and social factors are very well developed. Whales and dolphins, in fact, evolved such large brains millions of years before the brains of humans had reached the size they are today!

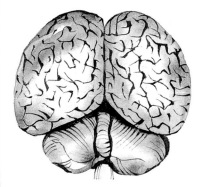
BRAIN OF A BOTTLENOSE DOLPHIN

Why do whales and dolphins sometimes strand themselves?

Sick and injured animals which are too weak to support themselves sometimes swim ashore so they don't drown, but healthy-looking whales and dolphins also sometimes strand themselves in large numbers. These mass deaths are not suicide, but rather unfortunate accidents which result when groups take the wrong route. Their biomagnetic sense usually maps out clear underwater 'highways' for them to follow, but some areas have confusing magnetic substances which form dangerous 'highways' headed straight for the beach. Cetaceans which live far out to sea are not as good at finding their way about close to shore and so strand more often than species which live closer inshore. Mass strandings of pilot whales seem to be the most common. Because they live in such close groups, they would rather all risk stranding themselves than desert a relative in distress.

Can whales and dolphins smell?

No, because the blowhole, or nostrils, of a cetacean are closed underwater and so they cannot detect different chemicals in the water. Toothed whales do have a sense of taste as they can detect different chemicals in their mouths using their taste buds. But, unlike some sharks and fishes, they are unable to detect these chemicals over a long distance in the water.

COMMON DOLPHIN

Finding food

The two different groups of cetaceans are both very well adapted for feeding on quite different types of food. The baleen whales use their baleen plates as a sieve to strain small animals from the water, while most of the toothed whales have lots of simple, cone-shaped teeth which they use to grasp slippery fish, squid and other prey.

RISSO'S DOLPHIN WITH OCTOPUS

What is a dolphin's favourite food?

Dolphins mostly eat fish and squid. Hake is a favourite fish on the menu of Heaviside's, dusky and striped dolphins, but smaller fish like anchovies and pilchards are preferred by common dolphins. And Risso's dolphin also has its own favourite food – squid and octopus! Squid is a popular choice on the menu of many of the other toothed whales, such as the sperm whale (see page 6). Although the much smaller pygmy and dwarf sperm whales also hunt squid in offshore waters, the young animals, always accompanied by their mothers, tend to feed in shallower inshore waters which they use as 'nursery areas'.

Do some whales have 'beaks'?

Yes, there are about 19 different species of beaked whales (see page 5) which live far out in the oceans. Their name comes from the fact that they all have a pointed snout which looks rather like a bird's beak! They are unusual because, like Cuvier's beaked whale, the males usually have only two teeth and the females appear toothless because their teeth never grow out of their gums. These rare creatures feed on squid and deepwater fish.

CUVIER'S BEAKED WHALE

Do baleen whales have any teeth at all?

No, they have instead a number of comb-like baleen plates which hang from the roof of the mouth and, quite unlike teeth, are made from a similar substance to the keratin in our finger nails. The large baleen whales, such as the blue whale, have hundreds of baleen plates which they use to feed on smaller prey than any of the other cetaceans! They eat mostly krill, tiny shrimp-like creatures that drift in the ocean in enormous swarms. A baleen whale takes a huge mouthful of water which contains krill and then uses its tongue to strain the water out through the spaces between the baleen. The food is trapped against the baleen plates and then licked off and swallowed. Although krill, a type of zooplankton, is the favourite food of the blue, fin and minke whales in the southern oceans, different zooplankton and even fish are eaten by other baleen whales such as the sei and Bryde's whale.

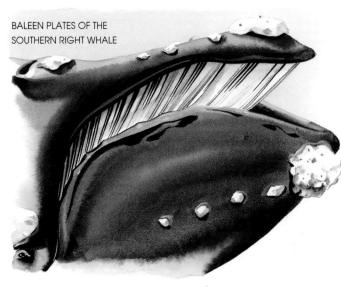

BALEEN PLATES OF THE SOUTHERN RIGHT WHALE

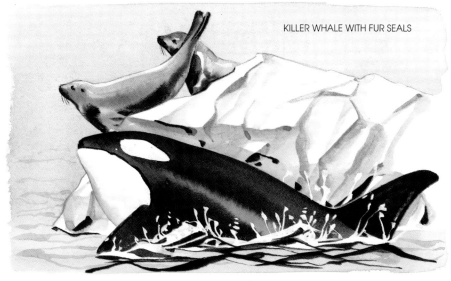
KILLER WHALE WITH FUR SEALS

Do killer whales really deserve their name?

Although killer whales sometimes eat warm-blooded animals such as seals, other whales and sea-birds, stories of their vicious natures and monstrous appetites are quite untrue. They are excellent hunters, but they are also gentle and loving towards one another. For this reason, many people prefer to call them orcas. They eat mostly fish and squid, but are quite fussy eaters and don't simply attack whatever swims past them. Rather, they eagerly search out and hunt their favourite food!

Can whales really fast for months on end?

Yes! Some of the large baleen whales such as the blue whale and the humpback whale obtain almost all their food needed for a whole year in the four summer months that they spend in Antarctic waters where food is plentiful. They then move further north to warmer waters and for the remaining eight months of the year they survive on fat reserves in their blubber, eating little or nothing throughout the winter months!

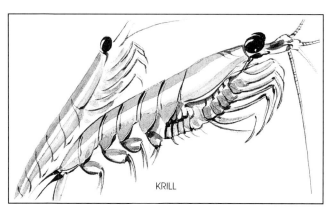
KRILL

Why do some whales have wrinkles on their throats?

Some baleen whales, such as Bryde's whale, have grooves in their throats, which make the throat look wrinkled. These whales are called rorquals. The grooves are used in much the same way that a pelican uses its pouch when feeding. When the whale feeds, these grooves fold out so that the mouth can hold more water – and more food, of course! Many tons of water can then be filtered with each mouthful and the whale can strain out enough food to fill its huge belly.

Did you know?

A blue whale's appetite is so big that it can eat as much as four tons of krill on a single summer's day! This means that about four million tiny shrimps are engulfed daily, making the massive blue whale one of the world's most formidable predators!

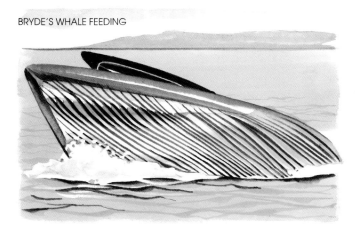
BRYDE'S WHALE FEEDING

Which whale has the biggest mouth of them all?

The biggest mouth in the cetacean world belongs to the bowhead whale which lives in the chilly Arctic seas and has baleen plates which are over four and half metres long! Right whales also have enormous mouths with two-metre long baleen plates. Bowhead and right whales both lack throat grooves and feed in the surface layers of the ocean by cruising through swarms of tiny zooplankton with their mouths open, 'skimming' the surface layers until enough food collects on their baleen plates to be licked off.

SEALS

Hunters of the high seas

Whales and dolphins use many different techniques to outsmart their prey and ensure that lunch arrives on time! These clever hunters often work together to herd their prey, and are known as co-operative hunters.

KILLER WHALE

Do killer whales ever come onto land?

Sometimes, to catch seals! In the waters of the Antarctic, killer whales gather around islands during the seal pupping season. There are then lots of seals on the islands and the killer whales sometimes swim right onto the beach to catch an unsuspecting seal! With the seal in their mouth, they then have to wiggle their way backwards into the water to enjoy their meal. Killer whales in these areas also tilt floating pieces of ice so that a sleeping seal or other prey animal slides down the ice and into the water or the waiting jaws of another whale.

Can whales 'fish' with lures?

Maybe. Some scientists believe that the shiny teeth of some toothed whales and the brightly coloured pink-and-white mouth of the killer whale and false killer whale may act as lures to attract fish and squid. It is also quite possible that the teeth of some deep diving whales glow in the dark because they have tiny, luminous creatures living on them and this may attract squid. The sperm whale may also have its own special way of attracting giant squid. As the whale hangs motionless in the water (see page 12), it can not only move its lower jaw up and down, but also from side to side, so that it looks like the tentacle of a giant squid!

Why do humpback whales blow bubbles underwater?

This is one of the most interesting feeding techniques of any cetacean! A humpback whale circles beneath a school of zooplankton or small fish and as the whale slowly rises it blows clouds of bubbles. These rise to the surface to form a 'bubble net' around the tiny prey so that they are trapped. The whale will then rise to the surface with its mouth wide open, and swallow the trapped parcel of food! Humpback whales may also swim in circles and use their tail flukes to herd their prey or even to stun them.

HUMPBACK WHALE 'BUBBLE-NETTING'

Why do dolphins sometimes gather in huge schools in the ocean?

Because the fish and squid they prey on are also found in large numbers! Their prey is widely scattered in the open ocean so large schools of dolphins have a better chance of finding food than one animal hunting alone or in a small group. Prey can also be herded more easily by a large group of dolphins. Large schools may provide protection from predators such as sharks and killer whales and provide the sociable dolphins with lots of company!

COMMON DOLPHINS
CHASING FLYING FISH

Do sperm whales sometimes battle with giant squids?

Not very often! Although male sperm whales often have large scars on their bodies, these are usually the result of fierce battles between adult male sperm whales, rather than life-and-death struggles with monstrous squids. But big sucker-shaped scars around the whale's head seem to tell a different story! These may well be caused by some of the giant deepwater squids which sperm whales prey on. The largest recorded squid eaten by a sperm whale was 19,5 metres (longer than most sperm whales!) and must have put up a fierce fight to resist being swallowed up whole! But most squids eaten by sperm whales are much smaller and weigh less than seven kilograms.

How do dolphins hunt for prey?

Dolphins will often co-operate in hunting by herding a school of fish and then taking turns to dash in and feed on the fish while the rest of the school guards the catch. While some dolphins such as Fraser's dolphin prefer to patrol waters far offshore for their meals, others such as the humpback dolphin feed on fish and cuttlefish very close inshore. Common dolphins are less fussy about where they hunt and will even chase flying fish on the surface by leaping right out of the water! Male and female dolphins may also feed in different ways: in bottlenose dolphins, for example, adult males hunt further offshore and feed on larger prey than the mothers and suckling calves.

Can some whales and dolphins really 'stun' their prey?

Yes! Many scientists believe that toothed whales such as dolphins and sperm whales are able to use a powerful low frequency blast of sound to stun prey. It is even thought that these sound waves not only stun prey, but also destroy parts of their body tissue, making squid and fish easier to catch! Dolphins use the fat deposits in the front of the head to focus and direct these shock waves towards their prey, while the sperm whale uses its massive spermaceti organ (see page 12).

SPERM WHALE

Sounds of the sea

Squawks, squeaks, barks, belches, groans, grunts and whistles – the seas are alive with the sounds of babbling whales and dolphins! From the quieter types like the blue whale to the more lively and chatty dolphins, they all have their own special way of sending their messages across the seas.

HUMPBACK WHALES

Why do humpback whales slap the water with their fins?

This may be a way of passing on a message or showing they are angry. Humpback whales and southern right whales sometimes chase killer whales away by loudly splashing the water with their fins and flukes. Other cetaceans do just the opposite when in danger and stop their noisy babblings as soon as a killer whale enters the area.

Do whales sing?

We think so. Humpback whales are famous for singing beautiful songs during the breeding season. The different populations sing different songs, with most male singers giving their best performances at night. Exactly why they sing these songs remains a mystery, but because it is only the males which sing, the tunes may be a kind of 'love song' to win the hearts of females! The whales change their tunes every year.

How do whales and dolphins 'speak' to each other?

Different cetaceans 'speak' different languages and use a wide variety of sounds to communicate. For example, while dolphins can be heard clicking, squawking, and whistling to each other, the great whales usually moan and belch! Humpback whales even grunt, yelp and snort at one another when feeding! Injured or frightened cetaceans may also send long distress signals. Sound travels very well underwater so that whales can hear each other over long distances, and often several kilometres. Some scientists believe that the sperm whale and humpback whale can communicate over even longer distances, perhaps even across whole oceans! To do this, they use 'sound-reflecting' layers of water about 1 000 metres down in the ocean which can carry sounds over extremely long distances.

How do cetaceans know who's who?

Just as we all have names, sperm whales each have a very special clicking call which can be used by other whales to identify another individual. Neighbours usually all have different names or 'signature' calls, but one sperm whale may have a similar 'name' to another in a different group. Some dolphins and killer whales also use 'signature' calls to tell them who's who in their own school.

KILLER WHALE
BREACHING

Do different whale groups 'speak' different languages?

Yes! Killer whales 'speak' to one another using a wide variety of clicks and whistles. Killer whales are found in most of the world's colder oceans but, just as with humans, pods (see page 24) speak different languages in different areas! Neighbouring pods usually speak the same language and if a foreign pod passes by, they do not mingle with these animals which produce a number of different sounds.

Can a dolphin learn to talk?

Although scientists have been trying for many years to find a dolphin 'language', they still cannot prove that dolphins are able to 'talk' in the same way humans do. Dolphins produce very different sounds to humans and these mean different things to the dolphins, so it is very difficult to 'translate' them into our own languages. But dolphins can understand the meaning of some sounds when trained to do so.

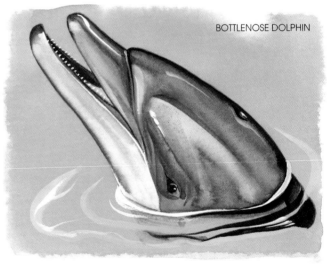

BOTTLENOSE DOLPHIN

Are whales acrobats?

Yes. Whales communicate not only by sounds, but by body language too. One of their most spectacular acrobatic stunts is called 'breaching'. They shoot their huge bodies backwards out of the water and then fall back in with a mighty splash that can be heard several kilometres away! Calves look quite funny as they splash around while learning to breach! No-one is sure why whales breach, but it may be a form of long-distance communication to let other whales know who's around, or they may simply be playing. Breaching can be quite 'infectious', with whale after whale joining in and trying to outdo the others as they perfect their acrobatics!

Did you know?

Toothed whales, such as the pilot whale, sometimes clap their jaws together loudly as a threat when they are angry. They may also show their anger or frustration by slapping the water with their tails.

SHORT-FINNED PILOT WHALE

21

Raising a family

Family life is as important to whales and dolphins as it is to humans, and dedicated mothers spend many hours fussing over their young, often with the help of other members in the group.

SOUTHERN RIGHT WHALE WITH CALF

Do calves suckle like human babies?

Not exactly. Although calves do suckle, in cetaceans the mother actually pumps milk into the calf's mouth so that it receives milk as quickly as possible from her teats. This is important because a new-born whale and dolphin would not otherwise be able to stay underwater long enough to get all the milk it needs.

Do whales ever kiss?

It seems so. Killer whales are very gentle when courting each other and may even nibble each others tongues, so it looks as if they are kissing! Whales court each other in different ways. Male humpback whales, for example, charm females by slapping the water with their long flippers or tail flukes, by rolling in the water or by leaping right out of the water (see page 21)! Some courting dolphins perform acrobatic stunts to attract females, such as leaping out of the water or even swimming at great speed.

Are whales born in nurseries?

Sometimes. A number of whales, including the southern right whale, use sheltered bays and other protected areas along the coast as nurseries where they can safely give birth to and care for their calves. Some of the favourite nurseries of the southern right whale include sheltered areas between False Bay and Algoa Bay in South Africa, in the Great Australian Bight and also off Warrnambool in Australia.

KILLER WHALES

Did you know?

A blue whale can produce as much as six hundred litres of milk in a single day! This milk is much richer than either human or cow milk because the mother has to give her rapidly growing calf as many nutrients as possible in a very short time, or else the calf would have to spend all its time suckling underwater.

Why are cetaceans born tail first?

So they don't drown! The birth of a young whale or dolphin takes place underwater, of course, and can last a few hours. If it was born head first the calf would be unable to breathe until it was free from its mother and may drown.

BOTTLENOSE DOLPHIN GIVING BIRTH

Do dolphins really have 'helping aunts'?

Yes, and so do whales. When a cetacean gives birth, there is very often another female, called an 'aunt', standing by to help the newborn calf to the surface so that it can take its first breath. Sperm whales sometimes have several aunts and they may form a protective circle around a young whale when danger threatens.

Can whales have twins?

Yes! In fact, they can even have triplets, but this is very rare and it is highly unlikely that all the calves will survive. Most whales and dolphins carry their unborn calf for about a year, and produce only one calf every two to three years. Female killer whales and pilot whales give birth to only four to six calves in a life-time, and stop breeding when they get older. This is rather unusual as most other whales breed throughout their adult life.

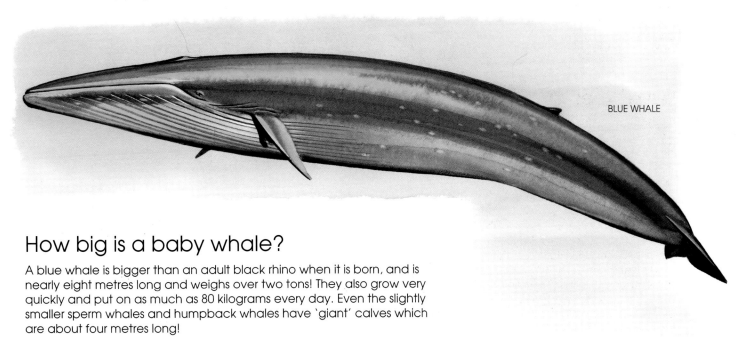

BLUE WHALE

How big is a baby whale?

A blue whale is bigger than an adult black rhino when it is born, and is nearly eight metres long and weighs over two tons! They also grow very quickly and put on as much as 80 kilograms every day. Even the slightly smaller sperm whales and humpback whales have 'giant' calves which are about four metres long!

Living together

Most whales and dolphins are quite social animals and often live together in big groups. In much the same way as elephants, they are well known for helping other members of their group who are injured and protecting one another from predators.

POD OF KILLER WHALES

What is a pod?

Killer whales live together in groups called pods. Pods contain up to about 50 animals, mostly family members, and these groups often stay together for life. Members of each pod stay close together and they not only help each other to hunt but also care for any sick or injured whales in their group.

Do dolphins go to school?

No, but they live together in groups called schools, which may consist of only a few dolphins or even thousands. Unlike the killer whales, which remain with their own pod, family groups of dolphins move from one school to another. The school provides protection from predators. Young dolphins are also able to copy and learn from the adults and it is easier for them to find food as a school than by hunting alone (see page 19).

Do cetaceans ever help each other?

Yes, two dolphins often help an injured member of their group by supporting it at the surface of the water so that it can breathe. Females are also very protective of their calves and some distressed mothers have been known to carry a dead or dying calf on their back for days or even weeks. Sperm whales will also support a dead calf for a while and will often help a sick member of their group. They do this by forming a tight protective circle around the injured whale, and they remain in this position with their heads facing inwards until the whale either dies or recovers. They may also do this to protect their young from killer whales.

How do some whales say hello?

Whales often greet one another or charm a mate by gently rubbing heads together or rubbing their head along the body of the other whale. Their thick blubbery skin is surprisingly sensitive to touch because it contains a number of nerve endings. Also, newborn whale and dolphin calves have sensitive bristles on their face which allow them to determine the best place to be carried along in the water flow next to their mother, before they can swim by themselves.

COMMON DOLPHINS

SPERM WHALE
WITH CALF

Why do sperm whales go to nursery school?

For some of the same reasons that humans do – they learn from adults, play with each other and are safe! Female sperm whales, juveniles and calves form nursery schools of about 25 animals to protect the young whales from predators such as sharks and killer whales, and also to share the duties of raising the calves. And a calf not only gets milk from its own mother, but also from other mothers in the nursery school! Sperm whale bulls usually only join nursery schools for a short time during the breeding season, when they mate with the females that do not already have suckling calves.

Do whales fight with each other?

Yes, some of the biggest fights in the animal world take place when massive 30 ton sperm whale bulls fight over females. They ram their huge heads together, and in the more serious fights the males may even lock their jaws together and wrestle, or tear out chunks of each other's flesh with their teeth! But the fights are usually just a threatening show of strength. No serious harm is done and the weaker whale soon gives up the fight.

Why does the male Risso's dolphins have scars?

The scars are caused by the teeth of the other male Risso's dolphins, mostly during fights over females. Although other whales and dolphins, including Blainville's beaked whale, also carry battle scars, those of Risso's dolphin are much more obvious so they are a useful way of identifying this large dolphin which grows to just over three meters long.

RISSO'S DOLPHIN

Do dolphins take turns to sleep?

Some certainly do – and for a very good reason! Spotted and spinner dolphins sometimes live together in groups. The spotted dolphins usually sleep at night and feed during the day. This means they are awake and on the look-out for danger during the day, which is when spinner dolphins like to sleep. And the spinner dolphins are awake during the night and keep a look-out while the spotted dolphins are asleep. In this way the two species take turns to protect each other and to get a good night's sleep!

SPOTTED DOLPHIN

SPINNER DOLPHIN

Living with others

Whales are so big that, to small creatures living in the ocean, they are a bit like islands which they can use as their homes! Being large also means that whales have very few predators, but the smaller dolphins are still sometimes preyed upon by sharks and killer whales.

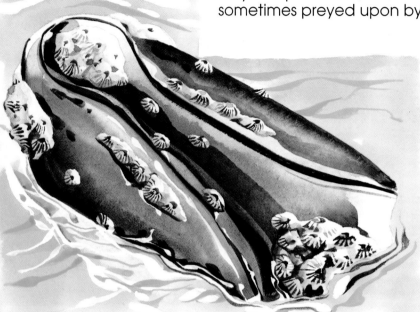

Do whales pick up hitch-hikers?

Yes! Small animals such as barnacles may attach themselves to the skin of a whale for a free ride. They do not harm the whale and are able to filter small food particles from the water as the whale slowly swims along. Because whales have no arms and fingers to scratch themselves with, they cannot remove uninvited guests and humpback whales may carry nearly half a ton of barnacles! Many of the barnacles prefer cold water and they drop off when the humpbacks migrate to warmer waters during the breeding season.

Have dolphins ever saved people from drowning?

Yes, there have been many cases where dolphins have saved a human life. One such rescue happened when a ship was wrecked just off the Mozambique coast. A young woman tried to swim toward land but, because she was injured, several sharks began circling her. Luckily, two dolphins arrived just in time to protect her and they helped her to a buoy where she could wait safely until the rescue teams arrived.

Are dolphins copy-cats?

Yes! Dolphins are excellent mimics and may copy the behaviour of many animals, including seals and turtles. Dolphins are playful and one mischievous bottlenose dolphin called Beaky was known to move anchors and boats around, and even tried to imitate swimmers and water skiers! A young dolphin in captivity in South Africa even imitated a human diver cleaning an underwater window by using a gull feather as a scraper!

Are ships ever attacked by whales?

Whales are normally very gentle and are not aggressive, but disturbed mothers with calves and angry sperm whales have both been known to attack ships. Sleepy sperm whales sometimes doze so deeply on the water's surface that ships bump into them quite by accident. In one case, a sleeping sperm whale was bumped and badly injured by a steamer, and as the whale lay in the water dying five of its companions arrived and rammed the steamer until it sank!

BOTTLENOSE DOLPHIN HELPING A SWIMMER

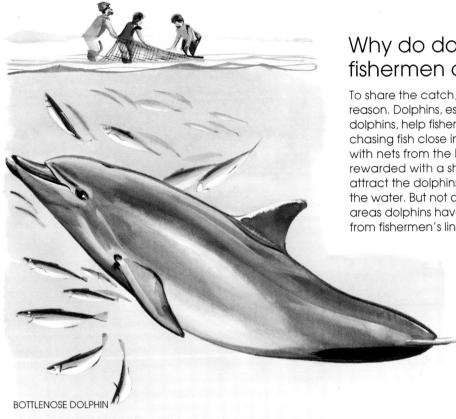

Why do dolphins help fishermen catch fish?

To share the catch, although this may not be the only reason. Dolphins, especially bottlenose and humpback dolphins, help fishermen in many areas of the world by chasing fish close inshore where they can be caught with nets from the beach. The dolphins are then rewarded with a share of the catch. The fishermen attract the dolphins' attention by slapping sticks on the water. But not all dolphins help fishermen. In some areas dolphins have become experts at stealing fish from fishermen's lines.

BOTTLENOSE DOLPHIN

How do dolphins trick others?

They have clever camouflage patterns. Many dolphins are dark-coloured above with lighter shades below, making it more difficult to see them from above against the dark ocean below, or from below against the bright surface of the water above. Other camouflage tricks include spots which make it easier for them to hide in dappled sunlight and stripes which make it harder for their prey to recognise the outlines of their bodies. Heaviside's dolphin also seems to 'cheat' because it has similar patterns on its belly to those on a killer whale. Predators will almost certainly hesitate to attack these dolphins if they look a bit like small killer whales!

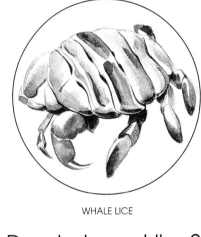

WHALE LICE

SPOTTED DOLPHIN

Do whales get lice?

Although whales don't get the same lice as humans, they do carry crab-like 'whale lice'. These are parasites which cling to the whale using their sharp claws and eat the whale's skin! Different species of whales carry different species of parasites. The pale patches which you may see on a southern right whale are actually huge groups of pale 'whale lice' which live among the folds of the whale's skin. They are also clearly visible between all the knobs and wrinkles on humpback whales.

Whale winners

BLUE WHALE

As big as a ship, as loud as a jet, and as quaint as a warthog – whales and dolphins hold some of the most astounding records in the animal world.

HEAVISIDE'S DOLPHIN

Who is the giant of the seas?

The blue whale not only earns the title of being the biggest cetacean, but it is also the largest animal ever to have lived on our planet,even dwarfing the great, extinct dinosaurs that once roamed the Earth. The sperm whale is the largest toothed whale and can grow to a massive 19 metres, while Baird's whale is the largest of the beaked whales and can grow to almost 13 metres.

Which is the smallest dolphin?

The smallest cetacean in the world is the Chilean black dolphin which grows to only about 1,2 metres. The other members of its group are almost just as small, growing to no longer than 1,8 metres, and include Heaviside's dolphin, Hector's dolphin and Commerson's dolphin. The smallest baleen whale is the pygmy right whale which grows to just over six metres.

Who makes the loudest noise?

The blue whale can make the loudest sound in the animal world, far louder than the roar of a lion! The loudest known whistle from a blue whale had a sound intensity of 188 decibels, but they seldom produce such loud sounds. Although the humpback whale does not make as loud a noise, it does tend to sing day and night during the breeding season, producing sounds as loud as a heavy-duty drill – between 100 and 110 decibels!

Which cetacean lives the longest?

It is very difficult to estimate how long a cetacean lives, especially because many of the whales which would have been quite old today were killed by whalers when they were still quite young. Most of the large baleen whales probably have life-spans similar to humans – one fin whale was estimated to have lived for over 80 years. The maximum possible age for a blue whale may be much more than this. Sperm whales live quite long – sometimes for more than 70 years. Some dolphins, like our bottlenose dolphins, can live for well over 40 years.

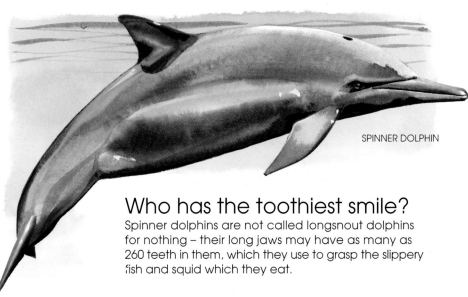

SPINNER DOLPHIN

Did you know?

A blue whale is so large that a dog could run along some of its blood vessels. It weighs about as much as 6 000 small children and a car could park in its mouth! It eats a million calories per day and only stops growing when it is between 25 and 30 years old.

Who has the toothiest smile?

Spinner dolphins are not called longsnout dolphins for nothing – their long jaws may have as many as 260 teeth in them, which they use to grasp the slippery fish and squid which they eat.

KILLER WHALE

Who is the real speed king of the seas?

The killer whale is probably the fastest cetacean, and can reach speeds of over 50 kilometres per hour in pursuit of prey. This is more than six times faster than human olympic swimmers, but well behind the fastest fish in the sea, the marlin, which can reach speeds of up to 80 kilometres per hour.

Which is our most beautiful dolphin?

Two of our dolphins are particularly striking: the common dolphin has a yellow and grey criss-cross pattern painted along its sides, and the southern right whale dolphin is beautifully marked in contrasting black and white.

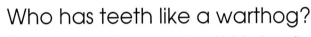

SOUTHERN RIGHT WHALE DOLPHIN

Who has teeth like a warthog?

The male Layard's beaked whale, which is also called the straptoothed whale, has two large teeth in the lower jaw which grow so large they almost meet on the top of the snout. The teeth in adult males form a strap over the jaws so that these odd creatures can hardly open their mouths! Scientists are still puzzling over how they manage to eat squid and other prey with their mouths strapped shut, and think that they probably have to suck them in! Blainville's beaked whale is just as strange – it has two raised teeth that look like horns!

Which is the fattest whale in our seas?

The stocky southern right whale: nearly half of its body weight is made up of blubber (see page 4)! Not surprisingly, this stocky whale is also one of the slowest swimmers, seldom even reaching speeds of ten kilometres per hour!

SOUTHERN RIGHT WHALE

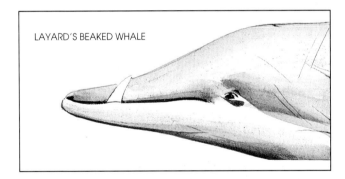

LAYARD'S BEAKED WHALE

HUMPBACK WHALE

Who has the biggest flippers of them all?

Humpback whales have flippers nearly five metres long! They sometimes lie on their side and wave one of their enormous white flippers in the air, perhaps as a means of greeting females in the area!

Save the whale!

Most countries have banned whale hunting, but many of the great whales are still endangered and not safe from extinction. Only about 500 of the 25 000 blue whales which once lived in Antarctic waters have survived. The smaller cetaceans are also in danger, and many thousands are killed by fishing nets and pollution every year.

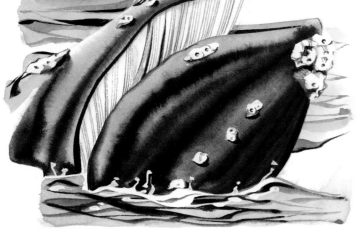

SOUTHERN RIGHT WHALE

Who is a whale's worst enemy?

Man. For centuries humans have hunted whales. Whales were an important source of food and materials for the early hunters like the Eskimos and the Basques of northern Spain. Toward the end of the nineteenth century, when better ships and harpoons were built, whaling became big business. Thousands of whales of all species and all around the world were killed until the great whales had almost disappeared. Luckily, man has not yet caused any whales to become extinct, but whales are still being killed by hunters in countries such as Norway and Japan. Man remains the whale's greatest enemy. We use dangerous fishing nets, and pollute their homes with poisonous chemicals, irritating noise and plastic wastes, all of which can harm whales.

How did the southern right whale get its name?

Because it was the 'right' whale to hunt – they swim slowly, float in the water when killed, and provide lots of oil and baleen. These whales were hunted so ruthlessly that a similar species, the northern right whale, is almost extinct today. The southern right whale has been a protected species since 1935 and today populations are thought to be slowly increasing, but it will still take many years before they recover.

SPINNER AND SPOTTED DOLPHINS CAUGHT IN A NET

Why were whales ever hunted?

Because one whale could provide enough products to fill a supermarket! Almost every part of the whale was used. Baleen was used as 'whalebone' in corsets, whips and brushes; whale skin was used as leather; ambergris from sperm whales was used to make perfume and whale oils were used to make soap, margarine and candles. Whale meat is eaten by people, and also sold as food for animals. Luckily these products can now all be made in ways which are much less destructive.

What is 'dolphin friendly' tuna?

This is tuna which has been caught, and then canned, without killing any dolphins. Fishermen in some parts of the world deliberately set their nets around spinner and spotted dolphins because there are usually tuna fish swimming close by. In the early 1970s as many as 300 000 dolphins became entangled and drowned in tuna nets in one year alone, and although the situation has now improved, thousands of dolphins are still killed in this way every year. Nets of all kinds hang like 'walls of death' in the water for dolphins, and many dolphins are killed every year in fishing nets or shark nets designed to protect swimmers.

STRANDED FALSE KILLER WHALES

What do I do if I find a dolphin stranded on the beach?

First get expert help from a museum or a marine research institute, for example, and make as many notes as you can about the stranding. Check that the dolphin's blowhole is not blocked and that no water can enter it. Dolphins can't sweat and so they overheat quickly. Keep the dolphin cool until it can be moved back into the sea by covering it (but not the blowhole!) with wet cloths, towels or even seaweed. Their skin is highly sensitive, so scoop holes in the sand for their flippers and flukes, and keep these wet too. Try not to frighten the dolphin with loud or excited behaviour. Remember, too, that only an expert should try to put a seriously injured whale or dolphin out of its misery – or the animal may not die immediately and may suffer even more.

Is it cruel to keep dolphins in captivity?

Many people believe that dolphins are unhappy in their small tanks which confuse their echolocation signals (see page 14), that they miss their mates and are easily bored. Other people argue that it is much easier to study dolphins in captivity and knowing more about them may help us to save them later. This is also the only way in which most people will ever be able to see these fascinating animals. Many of the world's large cities have dolphinaria and keep only small dolphins like bottlenose and dusky dolphins. But some big dolphinaria, like San Diego's Sea World, keep performing orcas as well and this is considered by many to be especially cruel.

DUSKY DOLPHIN

Who makes the laws to protect whales and dolphins?

The International Whaling Commission (IWC) makes most of the suggestions on how to protect the world's whales. In 1979 the IWC declared the Indian Ocean a sanctuary for whales, dolphins and porpoises, and they are also considering making the southern oceans a safe home for cetaceans. Not all countries belong to the IWC and follow its suggestions, but thanks to the long and brave struggles of conservation groups such as Friends of the Earth and Greenpeace, most countries have now banned whaling. Many countries, including South Africa and Australia, have laws to protect whales and dolphins within 320 kilometres of their coasts. Sadly, these laws do not protect dolphins from a dangerous invisible killer – poisonous chemicals such as pesticides which build up in their bodies, are transferred to their young and can result in fewer young being born, or even death. We need to stop marine pollution.

INTERNATIONAL WHALING COMMISSION

Could any whales become extinct?

Sadly, yes! Blue whales and northern right whales were once hunted so extensively that researchers are still unsure whether populations will ever recover. Because most of the great whales are now so scarce, whalers have started hunting the smaller minke whales. Although minke whales are still quite common, they have now become the world's most exploited whales.

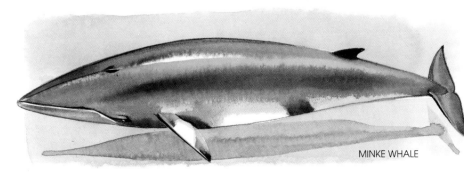

MINKE WHALE

Index

A
acrobatics 21
adaptation 10, 12, 14, 16
Antarctic 9, 18, 30
Arctic 17
Asia 5, 8
Atlantic Ocean 8
aunts 23
Australia 8, 22, 31

B
Baird's whale 28
baleen 3, **16**, **17**, 30
baleen whales 3, 5, 6, 16, 17, 28
barnacles **26**
beaked whales **5**, 12, **16**, 28, **29**
  Arnoux's **5**
  Blainville's 25, 29
  Cuvier's **16**
  Hector's 5, 9, 28
  Layard's 29
behaviour 4, 6, 10, 19, 20, 21, 24, 25, 26
bends 13
biomagnetism 115
birth 9, 22, **23**
blowhole 3, **6**, 7, 10, 11, **12**, 15, 31
blubber 4, 17, 24, 29
blue whale 3, 17, **23**, **28**, 30, 31
bottlenose dolphin 4, **7**, 8, 12, **15**, 19, **21**, **23**, **26**, **27**
bottlenose whale 13, 28
bowhead whale 17
brain 4, 11, 13, **15**
breathing 4, 11, **12**, 13, **21**, 23
breeding 7, 9, 10, 20, 22, 23, 24, 26, 28
Bryde's whale **7**, 8, **9**, 16, **17**
bubble-netting **18**

C
calf 4, 9, 16, 19, 21, **22**, **23**, 24, **25**, 26
callosites 6
Canada 8
captivity 26, 31
Chilean black dolphin 28
coloration 7, 9, 27, 29
Commerson's dolphin 28
common dolphin **7**, 13, **15**, 16, **19**, **24**
communication 15, 20, 21

D
diving **12**, 13, 26
dolphinaria 31

'dolphin friendly' tuna 30
dorsal fin 6, 7, 9
dusky dolphin 7, 16, **31**

E
echolocation 4, 14, 15, 31
extinction 28, 30, 31

F
fat 4, 19
feeding 4, 9, 16, **17**, 18, 19, 24, 28, 29
fin 6, **7**, 20
fin whale 28
fish 11, 15, 16, 17, 18, 19, 28

fishing 11, 27, **30**
flipper 4, 29, 31
food 4, 16, 17, 19, 24, 28, 30
fossil 27
Fraser's dolphin **4**, 19
Friends of the Earth 31

G
genital organs 4, **7**
Greenpeace 31
grooves **11**, 17

H
haemoglobin 13
Heaviside's dolphin 7, **9**, 16, 27, **28**
humpback dolphin **9**, 19, 27
humpback whale 3, **6**, 8, 9, **10**, 17, **18**, **20**, 22, 23, 26, 28, **29**
hunting 12, 14, 16, **17**, **18**, **19**, 24, 29, **30**

I
identification 6, 7, 20
Indian Ocean **8**, 31
Indo-Pacific humpback dolphin **8**
Indo-Pacific humpback whale 6
intelligence 3, 4, 15
International Whaling Commission 31
Ireland 8

J
Japan 8, 30
Jonah 5

K
killer whale 3, 5, 7, 8, **17**, **18**, 19, 20, **21**, **22**, 23, **24**, 25, 26, 27, **29**
  false 18, **31**
  pygmy **14**
krill 16, 17

L
lungs 10, 12, 13

M
Madagascar 8
magnetic fields 15
melon-headed whale **5**
Melville, Herman 5
migration 8, 9, 14, 15, 26
minke whale **31**
Moby Dick **5**
movement 11, 14, 15
Mozambique 8, 26
muscles 11, 13

N
Namibia 8, 9
nasal passages 10, **12**
nets 27, **30**
New Zealand 8, 9, 11
northern right whale 30, 31
Norway 30
nursery 16, 22, 25

O
oil 11, 30

P
Pakistan 27
parasites 27
patterns 6, 7, 9, 27, 29

Pelorus Jack 11
pilot whale 5, 6, 11, **15**, 21
  long-finned **11**
  short-finned **21**
plankton 9, 14
pod 6, 21, **24**
pollution 30, 31
porpoise 5, 31
porpoising 7, 10
predators 17, 24, 25, 26, 27
pygmy right whale 28

R
Risso's dolphin 11, **16**, **25**

S
scars 19, 25
schools 19, 24, 25
sei whale 7, 16
shark 7, 15, 25, 26, 30
size 6, 9, 10, 23, 25, 26, 27, 28
skin **4**, **11**, 27, 30
sleep 11, 25, 26
smell 15
sound 14, 19, 20, 21, 28, 31
South Africa 8, 9, 22, 31
South America 8
southern bottlenose whale **13**
southern right whale **6**, **8**, 10, **11**, **16**, 17, 20, **22**, **26**, **29**, **30**
southern right whale dolphin **29**
Spain 28
speed 11, 22, 29
sperm whale 3, 5, **6**, **7**, 8, **12**, 13, 16, 18, **19**, 20, 23, 24, **25**, 26, 28, 30
  dwarf sperm whale 16
  pygmy sperm whale 16
spermaceti organ 12, 19
spinner dolphin **10**, **25**, **28**, **30**
spotted dolphin 6, **25**, **27**, **30**
spy-hopping 14
strandings **15**, 30, **31**
streamlining **4**, 11
striped dolphin 6, **14**, 16

T
tail fluke 4, **6**, **11**, 18, 20, 21, 31
teeth 3, 5, 16, 18, 28, 29
temperature 9, 10, 11, 17, 26, 31
throat 17
toothed whales 3, 6, 12, 15, 16, 18, 21
touch 24

W
water pressure 13
weight 5, 28
whale lice **27**
whaling 5, 10, 28

Z
zooplankton 16, 17, 18

Answers
1. Bottlenose dolphin
2. Southern right whale
3. Pygmy right whale
4. Killer whale
5. Dusky dolphin
6. Humpback whale